Scroll of Agony **September 15** **1939** It is difficult to write, but I consider it an obligation and am determined to fulfill it with my last ounce of energy. I will write a scroll of agony in order to remember the past in the future. For despite all the dangers I still have hopes of coming out of this alive. ■ Yesterday was a day of horror and destruction. Between five o'clock and seven o'clock on the eve of Rosh Hashanah there was an air raid on the North Quarter, which is predominantly Jewish. From where I was, I could see with my own eyes all the horror that such a murderous attack can bring upon quiet residents, who in their innocence were busy preparing themselves for the approaching holiday. A rumor had spread that Hitler had ordered the cessation of air attacks. He was forced to do this by Stalin "the merciful," who threatened to "void" their pact unless attacks the peaceful civilian populace ceased. Despite my bitterness, I could not help smiling at this bit of "consolation." And immediately we were all shown the veracity of this rumor. ■ The enemy mercilessly poured his wrath on the Jewish quarter with incendiary bombs. We too experienced such a bomb at 22 Nowolipki Street, opposite where we are. The effect is like an earthquake. But worst of all is the chaos which follows among the victims. No one knows where he is running. Each one runs to a place that has already been abandoned by another as unsafe. Carrying babies and bundles, distracted and terrified people desperately look for a haven. Tens of thousands of broken refugees find themselves lost in a strange city. These people fill every courtyard and every stairway, and during the turmoil of the fires there are none more miserable. Afterwards you hear details that curdle the blood. Hundreds of families are left with nothing—their wealth has been burned, their apartments destroyed, their possessions lost. ■ How has Warsaw, the royal, beautiful, and beloved city become desolate! ■ *September 23* . . . I shall never forget September 23, the date of the Day of Atonement in 1939. The Germans deliberately chose that sacred Jewish holiday for an intensive bombardment of the Jewish district. In the midst of this bombardment a strange meteorological phenomenon took place: heavy snow mixed with hail began to fall in the middle of a bright, sunny day. For a while the bombing was interrupted, and the Jews interpreted the snow as a special act of heavenly intervention. Even the oldest among them were unable to recall a similar occurrence. But later in the day the enemy made up for lost time with renewed fury. ■ In spite of the danger, my father and a few other men who lived in our house went to the neighboring synagogue. After a few minutes one of them came running back, his tallith (prayer shawl) on his head, a prayer book in his hand, and so shaken that for some time he was unable to speak. A bomb had fallen upon the synagogue and many of the worshipers had been killed. Then, to our great joy, my father returned unharmed. White as chalk, and carrying his tallith crumpled under his arm, he told us that many of those who only a moment before had been praying at his side had been killed during the service. ■ That night hundreds of buildings blazed all over the city. Thousands of people were buried alive in the ruins. But ten hours of murderous shelling could not break the resistance of Warsaw. Our people fought with increased stubbornness;

even after the government had fled and Marshal Rydz-Smigly had abandoned his troops, men and women, young and old, helped in the defense of the capital. Those who were unarmed dug trenches; young girls organized first-aid squads in the doorways of the houses; Jews and Christians stood shoulder to shoulder and fought for their native land. ■ On the last night of the siege we sat huddled in a corner of the restaurant below our house. A few elderly Jews chanted psalms in tearful voices. My mother had wrapped us all in thick blankets to protect us from the tiny splinters that filled the air. When she herself stuck out her head for a moment, she was hit on the forehead by a splinter of shrapnel. Her face was covered with blood, but her wound proved to be only a small scratch. We realized that our shelter was a firetrap, so we set out for Kozla Street to find safer quarters with our relatives, stumbling over the mutilated bodies of soldiers and civilians as we walked. We found only the skeleton of a house rising above a huge cellar packed full of people lying on the concrete floor. Somehow or other they made room for us. Beside me lay a little boy convulsed with pain from a wound. . . . ■ *September 29, 1939* This is a topic fit for a classical eulogist, capable of creating a new expression to describe the magnitude of destruction. Beautiful Warsaw—city of royal glory, queen of cities—has been destroyed like Sodom and Gomorrah. There are streets which have been all but wiped off the face of the earth. Hundreds of houses have been destroyed by fire or changed into islands of rubble. Dozens of streets have turned into desolate heaps of gravel. All this happened on that bitter and unforgettable day, September 25. It is difficult to walk among the still smoldering and smoking ruins. Only long walls are left, walls that stand unsupported, endangering the passersby, for they are liable to fall at any minute. In the midst of the ruins thousands of human beings lie buried. This is the third day that the bodies of people who did not manage to escape are being pulled out from among the ruins. The members of the Burial Society collect the bodies and arrange them in piles to be taken to the cemetery. ■ There is no end to corpses of horses. They lie fallen in the middle of the street and there is no one to remove them and clear the road. They have been rotting for three days and nauseating all the passersby. However, because of the starvation rampant in the city, there are many who eat the horses' meat. They cut off chunks and eat them to quiet their hunger. There isn't a store that hasn't been burned or damaged and whose goods were not ruined or stolen. In this transitional period when there is no government authority, pillaging and robbery are committed in broad daylight everywhere, and have increased in those stores which were not emptied by their owners. Warm winter clothes are most often stolen. Storekeepers have been known to invite passersby in off the street to take what they want, since the merchandise would be ruined anyway. ■ And we are waiting for Hitler's army. Once again, woe to us! ■ After all the horrors that we have endured, we wait for Hitler's army as for the spring rains. We are without bread and without water. Our nerves are shattered from everything that has happened during the last awful days. In such a condition, our only desire is to rest a while, even if it is under Hitler's rule. ■ The Warsaw Diary of Chaim A. Kaplan, *translated from Yiddish.*

IN THE WARSAW GHETTO SUMMER 1941

PHOTOGRAPHS BY WILLY GEORG WITH PASSAGES FROM WARSAW GHETTO DIARIES

COMPILED AND WITH AN AFTERWORD BY RAFAEL F. SCHARF

APERTURE

WILLY GEORG, a professional
photographer, served in the
German army in occupied Warsaw.
On a summer's day in 1941
his superior issued him a pass
to take his Leica behind the walls
of the Warsaw Ghetto. The film
he exposed on that day remained
in his possession, unseen,
for fifty years; the photographs
now appear on these pages.

PASSAGES FROM DIARIES return
words to a people who can
never be silenced. Supplemented
by notices posted in the ghetto
and fragments from the Polish
Underground Press, the writing
spans the years 1939 to 1943.

In October 1939,
the Germans cordoned
off a section of Warsaw,
declaring it an open
"quarantine" area for
Jews. In November
1940 the Warsaw Ghetto
was sealed. Only Jews
with war-industry jobs
were permitted to
travel back and forth

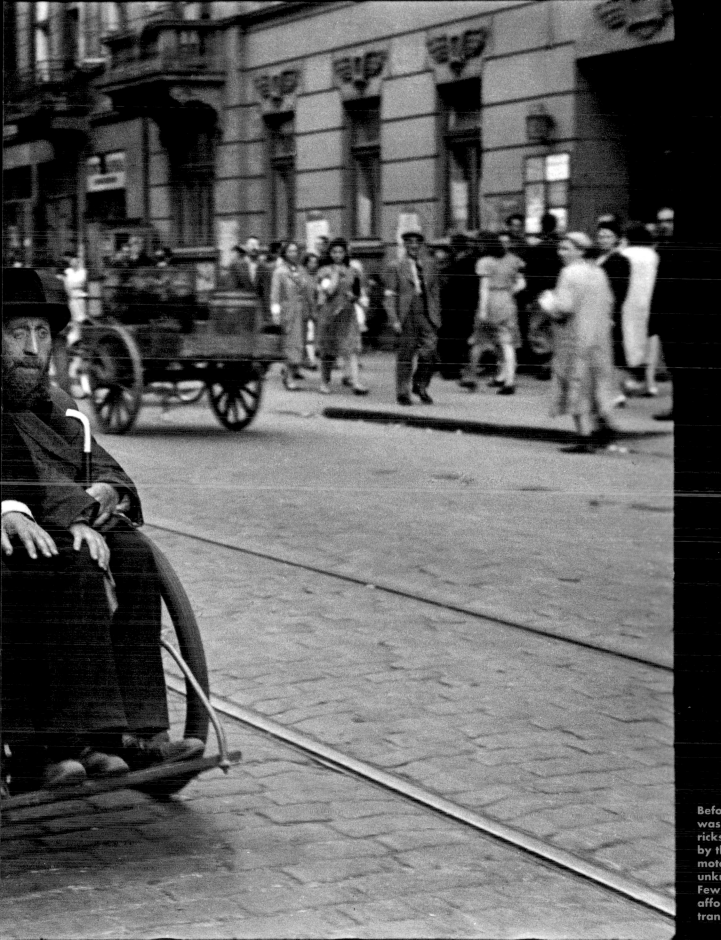

Before the ghetto was established, rickshaws—powered by the "human motor"—were unknown in Warsaw. Few Jews could afford this form of transportation.

Religious Jews with beards were subject to special harassment by the Germans, who often hacked the beards off. Soon bearded Jews went into hiding.

Star of David Near the newsstand there is a vendor of candy and cigarettes. He is an elderly man with the appearance of an intellectual. He is leaning against the wall, half slumbering. The candy he sells is made of molasses and saccharine in tiny ghetto factories. Sugar now costs thirty zlotys a pound. Some of the candies are wrapped in papers bearing the Star of David and the inscription "The Jewish Quarter." They cost from twenty to thirty groszy apiece. There is also candy which sells for a zloty for one piece. ■ Close by, an elderly woman at a little table sells arm bands of various qualities, from fifty groszy to two zlotys each. The cheapest are made of paper with a printed Star of David; the most expensive are of linen with a hand-embroidered Star of David and rubber bands. These arm bands are very much in demand in the ghetto because the Germans are very "sensitive" on this score, and when they notice a Jew wearing a crumpled or dirty arm band, they beat him at once. ■ Warsaw Ghetto: A Diary by Mary Berg, *translated from Polish.*

Arm bands were white
with a blue Star of David.
The Nazis required all
Jews to provide their own.
Some were purchased
and some homemade.
A stenciled one was a sign
of modest prosperity.

Arm-band peddler. On the wall is a sign for a paramedic. The ghetto had as many as 800 doctors, but few medical supplies.

Music and Song   There is music and song at every step: on the streets, in the courtyards, in the squares. They sing splendid operatic arias, and Polish and Yiddish songs. There are wonderful voices which [have performed] on the concert and operatic stage. . . . Cantors from synagogues large and small, former choristers and ritual butchers sing Hebrew synagogue songs. The ordinary street singers who have no voice and cannot sing, sing strange songs of their own composition. ■ The same happens with the courtyard music. Real musicians play here: professors from the schools of music and famous violinists from the Philharmonic orchestra and from the opera. And the most ordinary scraping of violins, plucking of zithers, and playing of empty bottles can also be heard. This procession continues through the courtyards from morning until late at night in spring, summer, and autumn. Most residents show their appreciation and gratitude. Apart from the theaters and musical cafés, this is how the residents' need for entertainment is satisfied. ■ *Jan Mawult, Diary written in the Warsaw Ghetto, Archives of the Jewish Historical Institute, Warsaw, translated from Polish.*

The average ghetto resident was able to get four pounds of bread per month. Dough was often mixed with sawdust or potato peels.

The Other Side And yet, there welled up within us a longing for the "other side," for the near and for the far away, for the strange and also for the familiar, and for our Polish friends and acquaintances. Thrown into the ghetto from a Poland whose name had been erased from the map of Europe but not from people's hearts, the attachment which we felt to our country and our nation was all the greater because their misfortunes were the direct cause of our own. And beyond the ghetto, beyond Warsaw and the whole of Poland, our desires, thoughts, and feelings joined with the whole world of free people fighting for the freedom of that world against the greatest tyrant in history. Shut up in the ghetto, we looked longingly at the streets of "Aryan" Warsaw, visible through the opening in the walls and from the windows of the houses bordering on them. We looked longingly at the "Aryan" streets and at the people walking along them without arm bands. ■ *Henry Makower,* The Cup is Filling, *Diary, Archives of the Jewish Historical Institute, Warsaw, translated from Polish.*

A life of the mind
sustained the ghetto.
Even with little money
for food, books
were bought and sold.
Typhus and lice
warnings are posted
on the wall.

Sugared Almonds The inferno of the ghetto. People are locked up, deprived of any opportunity to work or do something, people who have been branded, persecuted, and condemned to torment and death. And some of these people raise their heads and start doing something. In the ghetto, there is money, there are goods, there are craftsmen, and suddenly something unexpected happens: the ghetto begins to lead a life of its own. Barter starts up, and import and export. There are bodies in the street, typhus, an unheard-of mortality rate, and at the same time there is industry. Our ghetto starts supplying the whole of Poland with products and goods which they do not make themselves. Factories spring up like mushrooms after the autumn rains. Factories—if that is what one can call the little basements, the small rooms in which the most beautiful hosiery, stockings, knitwear, and socks are made. And workshops, where old sheets and pillowcases are dyed, patterned, and turned into the most fashionable men's shirts, beautiful floral head-scarves, and handkerchiefs. Chocolate with almonds produced from sugar, without cocoa or nuts. Tanneries and turning shops operate, there is mass production, and huge bribes are paid to the militia, plainclothes policemen, and Germans. ■ There are days when, despite this, machines and goods are removed and people taken away. One factory is closed down but two open up to provide people with work and a livelihood. We have beggars but there are also people who have money. Admittedly, they are a small handful but if one person has money, then another can always earn his keep from him and provide a livelihood for someone else. ■ And that is how the restaurants, nightclubs and open-air cabarets started up. There are the gray walls of the ghetto, starvation and death at every step, but in the basements there are places of amusement. L'Ourse ("The bear"). The glistening brilliance of mirrors and marble, of silver and crystal. Our excellent musicians play and the stars perform new acts as well as their old ones. The young singer with the voice of a nightingale sings so beautifully that it is as if the ghetto never existed, as if nobody knew what a German was. On a tray, they serve coffee and cakes or a tasty, scented pink mousse, and sugared almonds. ■ And later, when you go out from the lovely, brightly lit room into the dark street and two words reach your ears, "hot rachmunes" ("have pity"), and you see the emaciated body wearing rags, then you rue the pleasant moment spent in the nightclub, call yourself a heartless brute and realize that people can listen to music and songs, they can luxuriate in the warmth and the brightness but they can no longer dance. So, nobody dances in our nightclubs. Clearly, the line has to be drawn somewhere.
■ *Noemi Szac-Wajnkranc, Diary, translated from Polish.*

By March 1941, 66,000 additional Jews from the Warsaw district had been "resettled" in the ghetto. One of every three ghetto Jews was a refugee.

Broken window glass—
shattered by bombs
and vandalism—could
not be replaced.
Often iron gates were
the only barrier
between inside and
outside. A year later,
stores no longer
existed in the ghetto.

Answered by Fear The policemen used to tell people about letters from those who had been resettled, and yet no one had ever seen those letters. We wanted to believe them so that it would be easier for us to help with the resettlement. We did not want evidence that we were sending people to their deaths. The Germans used to kill the elderly so that we could believe that they would let the young and those fit for work live. . . . We suspected something but could not find out anything from the railway men. We did not know where they were sending these people. Was it possible for such old trains to reach as far as Bobruysk or Kiev? We made a note of the numbers of the departing railway wagons. After two hours, the same ones were back again, already empty. Where were they getting rid of their huge human loads? Near Warsaw, close to Malkina? There were thousands of people but nobody had seen them there or even heard of them. They would have had to use the whole army to shoot them. And who would have buried them? After all, some information would have got through to the neighboring villages. It would already be talked about in Warsaw! There is some terrible secret in all this. Somebody lets slip the word "Treblinka." You ask about it and are answered by fear. ■ I saw how they brought groups for transportation out of the cauldron on Mila Street. An SS man leapt around them like a monkey and beat them with a whip. He was cackling devilishly and shrieking in Polish: "Into soap, into soap, everyone's going to be turned into soap." . . . They took away whole teams of workers, entire functioning "workshops," together with their management. They took everyone to the wagons. They also loaded up the sick from the hospitals. We had been deceived. Instead of opposing them, we abetted the crime. ■ *Eugenia Szajn-Lewin,* In the Warsaw Ghetto, *Archives of the Jewish Historical Institute, Warsaw, translated from Polish.*

As food grew increasingly scarce, many ghetto residents were reduced to eating soup of wheat husks and rancid oats.

When the Germans invaded Poland, Warsaw was a thriving cultural center. Jews were believed to have been in Warsaw from the thirteenth or fourteenth century.

"Are You Jewish?" The child of the ghetto knows what a labor camp is, understands the meaning of raids, typhus, starvation, and refugee centers, and can show you where the Jewish prison is. If it has dolls, it stands them up against the wall and asks, "Bist du Jude? Bist du Jude?" ("Are you Jewish? Are you Jewish?") or shouts, "Hände hoch, Jude!" ("Put your hands up, Jew!"). Only privileged children go to play in the little gardens. Most children do not play or go to school. The Jewish child knows that it has to work, earn a living and sometimes take care of the whole family. The ghetto child does not laugh: it has already forgotten how. On its face is an adult scowl and it feels the bitterness of the wronged. Childhood does not exist. ■ Older children fill the streets. They earn something as peddlers, with their wares hung around their necks, as street singers, and as members of swift gangs of smugglers, secret suppliers of forbidden goods (white bread, flour, meat, sugar). Children work in the manufacture of brushes, mattresses, and toys. They sneak out of the gates of the ghetto, they smuggle and beg. They have terribly swollen limbs and faces—the swelling of starvation. The bodies of children [lying in the streets] are an everyday sight. . . . The death toll rises higher and higher. The monthly totals [between January and August 1941] are 450, 800, 1,200, 2,000, 2,500, 4,000, 5,600. Their faces get more and more sunken, their complexions paler and paler. . . . ■ *Jan Mawult, Diary written in the Warsaw Ghetto, Archives of the Jewish Historical Institute, Warsaw, translated from Polish.*

Jewish Policemen I experience a strange and utterly illogical feeling of satisfaction when I see a Jewish policeman at a crossing—such policemen were completely unknown in prewar Poland. They proudly direct the traffic—which hardly needs to be directed, for it consists only of rare horse-driven carts, a few cabs, and hearses. The latter are the most frequent vehicles. From time to time Gestapo cars rush by, paying no attention whatsoever to the Jewish policeman's directions. ■ Warsaw Ghetto: A Diary by Mary Berg, *translated from Polish.*

Jewish Policemen *November 15, 1942*

The Jewish police had a very bad name even before the resettlement. The Polish police didn't take part in the forced-work press gangs, but the Jewish police engaged in that ugly business. Jewish policemen also distinguished themselves with their fearful corruption and immorality. But they reached the height of viciousness during the resettlement. They said not a single word of protest against this revolting assignment to lead their own brothers to the slaughter. The police were psychologically prepared for the dirty work and executed it thoroughly. And no people are wracking their brains to understand how Jews, most of them men of culture, former lawyers (most of the police officers were lawyers before the war), could have done away with their brothers with their own hands. How could Jews have dragged women and children, the old and the sick, to the wagons knowing they were all being driven to the slaughter? There are people who hold that every society has the police it deserves, that the disease—cooperation with the Occupying Power in the slaughter of 300,000 Jews—is a contagion affecting the whole of our society and is not limited to the police, who are merely an expression of our society. Other people argue that the police are the haven of morally weak psychological types, who do everything in their power to survive the difficult times, who believe that the end determines the means, and the end is to survive the war—even if survival is bound up with the taking of other people's lives. ■ In the presence of such nihilism, apparent in the whole gamut of our society, from the highest to the lowest, it is no surprise that the Jewish police executed the German resettlement orders with the greatest of zeal. And yet the fact remains that most of the time during the resettlement operation the Jewish police exceeded their daily quotas. That meant they were preparing a reserve for the next day. No sign of sorrow or pain appeared on the faces of the policemen. On the contrary, one saw satisfied and happy individuals, well-fed, loaded with the loot they carried off in company with the Ukrainian guards. ■ *Emanuel Ringelblum, Notes from the Warsaw Ghetto, Archives of the Jewish Historical Institute, Warsaw, translated from Polish.*

Men were required to doff their hats to a German soldier and step off the sidewalk.

Along with rickshaws
and a few horses,
Jewish trollies provided
the only transportation.
All automobiles
had been requisitioned
by the Germans.

Horse-drawn
hansom cabs
transported people
and goods.
Soon horses were
to disappear.

In December 1941,
the Nazis made
all Jews relinquish
their furs.
A fur collar on a
coat would no
longer be seen.

The trolley was for Jews only, and stopped at the ghetto walls. This trolley ran along Grazybowska Street, "the street of mushrooms."

BLACKMAIL We were afraid that it might be too late. We walked up to the first Jewish policeman who came into sight and asked if we could get across to the "Aryan side." It turned out that we could but that it would cost 600 zlotys per head. We agreed and gave him the money. The stranger disappeared and, for a moment, we were afraid that the money had vanished. After a few minutes, he returned. He pulled a face when he heard that we did not have any documents but told us to follow him. . . . ∎ Just by the crossing itself, he told us to hide our armbands. He moved aside and we approached the Polish policeman who asked, "Where are you going?" The other one made a sign saying, "It's all arranged." We walked past and found ourselves in an empty street on the "Aryan side." We were overcome by strange feelings: triumph at the ease of the crossing and fear of what was yet to come. we tried not to walk too quickly so as not to attract attention. We realized that we looked strange: we were hot, out of breath and bareheaded, and we were carrying our coats over our arms. We could feel how the veins stood out on our temples and that we were being watched. We wanted only to hide in any nook or cranny so that we could have a rest and cool down but we were afraid to go into a doorway. We wanted to get as far away as possible from the blasted sentry outside the ghetto. We wondered whether to get on a tram but were also afraid to do that. . . . Approaching Chlodna Street we suddenly sensed that somebody was following us. . . . All of a sudden we were surrounded by a group of about ten teenagers between the ages of fourteen and sixteen. They started pulling at us from all sides and saying that they would go to the German sentry and hand us over to them unless we paid them off. Their faces were hideous. The majority were girls and they were the loudest and most aggressive. The most daring wanted to snatch our briefcases, and the rest, seemingly cheated, called out, "Why did you give them everything? Now give us some money or we will go and get the Germans." They pulled us into a doorway. We took out some money, a

couple of hundred zlotys, and started to divide it up. There was not enough to go around because more and more of them kept appearing. They wanted to snatch my wife's handbag. We told them that it was empty and, somehow, they left it alone. They tore her coat from her arm instead, and one girl tried to pull a ring from her finger. We assured them that is was of little value, that is was a memento, but it was no use. One of the boys was yelling that he had not gotten anything but we did not have any more money to hand over and we eventually broke away from them. They still ran after us and there was hardly any reaction from the people. Maybe they were frightened to say anything because it was so close to the sentry post. Only one old lady started to shout at them to leave us alone. She came up and asked us what they had taken and where we wanted to go. We could see that she felt sorry for us and might have hidden us but we did not want to endanger her, and besides, we wanted to get as far away as possible. Her compassion raised our spirits and the whole incident did not seem so awful to us. ∎ We returned to Wronia Street and walked across Kazimierz Square into Zlota Street. All of a sudden we had an awful feeling in our bones that somebody was watching us. We heard footsteps behind us. We turned into Zielna Street and were approached by two youngsters with suspicious faces who whispered, "Into the doorway!" We went into the doorway and several more of them appeared. The first demanded five hundred zlotys. We went up to the landing. We could hear the porter sweeping the stairs above. The gang wanted us to hurry up. We pulled out a couple of hundred zlotys from a side pocket and went downstairs. At this point, another stranger who looked like an informer with briefcase in hand appeared and pretended to check what was going on. This character frightened us the most. The "fee" had to be increased because it was to be shared with him. Some shadier characters appeared and the whole episode ended by them extracting a significant sum from us. In exchange they offered to escort us to wherever we wanted to go,

but we were afraid that they would try to blackmail us again. We wanted to get away from them as quickly as possible so that they would not be able to follow us or see where we were going. We ran out of the doorway. After a moment, a lad came up to us and said, "A dog is following you." . . . On the corner, we were approached by two teenagers, one of whom had a typically criminal, drunken face. He said in a whisper, "Please follow me to No. 1 Krolewska Street." . . . It was a new blackmail attempt and even more dangerous because they were not even talking about money but taking us to some house on Krolewska Street. We supposed that a Gestapo agency or something of that sort was situated there. This time we suggested that we should go into a doorway. . . . Finally they said, "Two thousand zlotys and not a penny less." We said that we did not have that much left. One became enraged and the other calmed him down and restrained him. We pulled out the rest of the money (there was still more than 1,000 zlotys). They haggled with us for several minutes, threatening us with Krolewska Street every minute, but in the end, they took the money and calmed down. We asked them if the blackmail was over, if they would follow us any further. They gave their word of honor that they would not. Even the one with the drunkard's face tried to reassure us. We got the impression that he was the sort of hooligan with whom one could come to some sort of agreement and we suggested to him ourselves that he should accompany us for a while in order to prevent further extortion. The trust that we exhibited flattered him. . . . They escorted us politely up to the Powisl and finally bade us a warm farewell, wishing us luck. From afar, we saw that they had gone. Only then did we go on and enter a café. ∎ We were terrified by the triple blackmail. We were convinced that it was not yet the end, that somebody was still lying in wait for us . . . every passerby was eyeing us suspiciously. Only after a couple of hours did we calm down but we were haunted for some time. . . . ∎ *Adolf and Barbara Berman, translated from Polish.*

Smuggling Another category of smuggler—motivated not by profit but rather by the satisfying of their families' needs—consisted of little children, often between six and seven years old, who slipped out of the ghetto "gates" unnoticed when the military police were busy checking the identity papers of people and carts passing through, or sneaked under the barbed wire . . . which cut off those parts that had not yet been walled in. ■ Those who saw these dwarfs laden with potatoes in their trouser legs and under blouses that were tied up at their waists, or in the turned-up hems of their coats, bent beneath the excessive weight, looking like shapeless figures, and had a ghastly smile evoked by this sight, had it wiped abruptly from their faces when they saw the moment that such a heroic little boy or girl crept back through the "gate" like a fox, was shot at from behind, and fell with a look of horror painted on their faces into their mother's arms nearby. . . . The mother had to collect herself straight away so that the military policeman standing close by should not notice the touching scene and guess its cause. Apart from that, the maternal hug could increase the pressure against the slip of a child's body of the potatoes hidden under its blouse. . . . ■ This host of children included within its wartime ranks beggars who got out beyond the ghetto walls, succeeded in begging a few groszy and used them to buy some bread or potatoes—the objects that they smuggled in. ■ The smuggling had the effect of alleviating hunger in the ghetto but did not reduce the mortality amongst those poor people who did not have the means to buy a piece of bread or some potatoes. ■ *Henryk Bryskier, Diary, Archives of the Jewish Historical Institute, Warsaw, translated from Polish.*

A street child wore what he could find, tying rags around his legs to fashion trousers.

Typhus, Typhoid, and Tuberculosis

In the summer of 1941 an epidemic of typhus, which had been preceded by numerous but sporadic cases, broke out with full force and was to rage with undiminished vigor for almost a whole year—until the spring of 1942.
■ It claimed tens of victims daily and reached two hundred victims a day at its height during October, November, December, and January. The mortality statistics show totals of six thousand recorded deaths for each of these months. And how many more of the buried were unregistered, nameless, utterly destitute gentlefolk who died on the streets from starvation and cold, and were buried in communal, unmarked graves in the Jewish cemetery? . . . ■ Poverty, starvation, and transportation to the camps struck at the poorest and weakest. But typhus was more democratic. It claimed victims from all strata, spheres, and professions. By a strange twist of fate, the most needy were more resistant to this illness than the well-to-do, who had been the likely victors of this economic war.
■ Typhus had been the legal pretext for the regulation setting up the Jewish residential district, but there was no typhus then, and if there had been a small epidemic of typhoid fever in the autumn and early winter of 1939, then it affected Poles and German soldiers as much as Jews. ■ Typhoid fever was produced precisely by those walls, within which a mass of half a million impoverished and starving people had been rounded up and crammed, half of whom were forced to live in filthy conditions for a prolonged period (because for a long time there was no permission given for the removal beyond the walls of waste and refuse). ■ Is it surprising that lice found fertile breeding grounds in such conditions? . . .
■ The fight against the epidemic was launched. Despite the lack of help and medication from outside, the quarantining of refugees, the regular "steaming" of flats, houses, and whole blocks, and the disinfection of homes,

possessions, and people were organized. The latter was carried out by mobile disinfection teams armed with gas and protective clothing. A number of public baths were opened, and at lectures, on posters, on the streets, in offices, and in homes, there were exhortations to cleanliness. . . . Every case of typhus had to be reported to the Health Department, the dwelling immediately disinfected and the patient taken to the hospital. Treatment was never given at home—on pain of death for the doctor. There was no more room for the sick in the hospitals. All wards had to give way to the one for infectious diseases. On each of the four hospitals in the ghetto . . . hung a warning notice: "Seuchkrankenhaus!" ("hospital for infectious diseases"). Every second gate was locked, with a yellowing warning on it and a policeman on guard outside, while inside a "steaming" was being carried out. In the streets, there were processions of people being escorted by the police into quarantine and to the baths for a "steaming."
■ It seemed as if those who had not died of poverty and starvation, or even of the cold as a result of the harsh winters and the regulation confiscating all fur garments, would be finished off by contagion. Instances of cholera and bubonic plague have already been mentioned. . . . As a result of the fight against it, and also of its spontaneous extinction, the epidemic died down at the beginning of spring 1942. It died out only to be replaced by a new disease which made terrible progress from then on, above all amongst the children. The latter, who had been so resistant to typhus, died like flies of tuberculosis. Around 30,000 people died of typhoid fever and about 200,000 fell ill with this disease [tuberculosis], which required such expensive medication to fight it. Proportionally, the largest number of victims came from the medical profession.
■ *Stefan Ernest, Diaries, Archives of the Jewish Historical Institute, Warsaw, translated from Polish.*

Symptoms
of starvation
included not
only emaciation,
but often
swollen limbs.

"I Thank You God . . ." One family from Lodz, consisting originally of eight people, was well-known. All that they possessed were the two prams in which he wheeled three children and she two. They pushed the prams [along] the road and sang old Yiddish songs. They had lovely voices. She sang and he sang, and they were accompanied by six childish trebles; then there were four, then there were three and one pram disappeared, and their shoes, and the remains of their outer clothing disappeared. Recently, the family consisted of two people and one pram. Both he and she lay in the pram. She was thirty-nine but looked a hundred, and accompanied her husband. They sang the same songs and received the same pittance as last year. ■ Another well-known character, standing out from the gray mass of those dying beneath the walls of the houses, was Nuchem Lejbkorn. Before the war, he had owned a house and had a shop, a wife, and five children in Skierniewice. The Germans resettled him in Warsaw. Within a couple of months, he became a beggar. His wife died of typhus. The eldest child died in the same week. He moved from a sublet room to a refugee center and, from there, onto the street. They walked the streets of the ghetto. Three children held onto the remains of his suit and he carried the fourth on his shoulders. He walked and sang only one Yiddish song, "Ich dank dir Got, az ich bin a id" ("I thank you God that I am a Jew"). Then the children died of starvation. But he was still strong, he still walked about although his legs were already swollen. Autumn passed and he was still walking about, then winter, and he was already shoeless and naked. He had a quilt left, which he walked around in, tied up with string, with his hands inside. From beneath the quilt protruded his terribly swollen legs, and from above, a small, desiccated, yellow-skinned, pinched face, bordered by a pointed beard. Feathers spilled from the quilt. Because of this, passersby gave him a wide berth on the crowded streets. One or another threw a couple of groszy into the tin attached to him by string and he walked on through he middle of the crowd, happy, with a smile on his imbecile's or philosopher's lips and always singing the same song: "Ich dank dir Got, az ich bin a id." ■ *Samuel Puterman, Diary, Archives of the Jewish Historical Institute, Warsaw, translated from Polish.*

Money played an important part in the survival rate. Ghetto residents were very quickly reduced to a few shabby clothes, as they sold off what they had to buy food.

New Faces A special class of beggars consists of those who beg after nine o'clock at night. You stand at your window, and suddenly see new faces, beggars you haven't seen all day. They walk out right into the middle of the street, begging for bread. Most of them are children. In the surrounding silence of night, the cries of the hungry beggar children are terribly insistent, and, however hard your heart, eventually you have to throw a piece of bread down to them—or else leave the house. These beggars are completely unconcerned about curfews, and you can hear their voices late at night, at eleven and even at twelve.

They are afraid of nothing and of no one. There has been no case of the night patrol shooting at these beggars, although they move around the streets after curfew without passes. It's a common thing for beggar children like these to die on the sidewalk at night. I was told about one such horrible scene that took place in front of 24 Muranowska Street, where a six-year-old beggar boy lay gasping all night, too weak to roll over to the piece of bread that had been thrown down to him from the balcony. ■ *Emanuel Ringelblum,* Notes from the Warsaw Ghetto, *Archives of the Jewish Historical Institute, Warsaw, translated from Polish.*

Clinging to Life

One of the most remarkable incidental phenomena seen in the present war is the clinging to life, the almost complete cessation of suicides. People are dying in vast numbers of the typhus epidemic, are being tortured and murdered by the Germans in vast numbers, but people do not try to escape from life. In fact just the contrary: people are bound to life body and soul and want to survive the war at any price. The tension of this epoch-making conflict is so great that everybody, young and old, great and small, wants to live to see the outcome of this giant struggle, and the new world order. Old men have only one wish: to live to see the end and to survive Hitler. ■ I know an old Jew, gray with age, about eighty years old. This old man was hit by a terrible misfortune last winter: he had an only son, aged fifty-two, who died of typhus. He had no other children. The son is dead. He hadn't remarried and had lived together with his son. A few days ago I visited the old man. As I was saying goodbye to him (he is still in complete command of his faculties), he burst into tears and said to me, "I want to live to see the end of the war and then live for just another half-hour longer." ■ We may well ask: what has such an old man to live for? But he does have something. He too wants to live for "just half an hour" after the last shot is fired, and this is the passionate desire of all Jews. ■ *Abraham Lewin, A Cup of Tears, translated from Yiddish and Hebrew.*

It is 4 AM on the night of the 6th of January. I am woken by noise from the adjoining rooms, the stairs, and the courtyards. The neighbors tell me that all Jews are to collect in the roads adjoining the Umschlagplatz by 10 o'clock. . . . ■ It looks like the end of the six-week-old "game" with the Jews of Warsaw. The panic amongst the people is indescribable. . . . They have lost their heads and no longer know what to do. . . . In the courtyard, an older man (over fifty) who has more experience of life than I do stops me and asks despairingly what he should do now. ■ However, the greatest surprise is the fact that members of the Jewish police force, who have hitherto been safe and immune from such roundups, must also leave their block and gather in Wolynskia Street. Their families, protected until now, drag bundles in that direction. But the Jewish police force is still full of self-confidence and believes to the last that it will survive. ■ 6 AM. The streets, hitherto deserted, now teem with people . . . only four hours left. The sight is frightening. The things that make the most awful impression on me are the bundles, the packages, the bedding, and the old furniture. People are still so full of hope that "perhaps somehow. . . . " ■ Countless throngs stream along the street. . . . Here and there, groups of people have already settled down in the road, on the burnt-out ruins of houses—real encampments. Particular "workshops" already occupy the buildings "designated" for them. . . . ■ My "workshop" gathers on the ruins of a burnt-out building. The mood of the people is changeable. At moments, it is like before an impending raid. At other times, it is if people are only going to an allocation of barracks. The people look around the new flats and complain about the lack of water, toilets, and electricity. The day before, there was a terrible raid, which had simply decimated our "workshop." Amongst those present are lots of injured families, and they are deeply depressed. The people are generally worn out, it is sweltering hot, and there is no water. ■ About midday, the German proprietors of the factories arrive. There is a mood of expectation. People are already utterly exhausted. They would agree to live in the worst hovels, several families squeezed in together, merely to stay alive. Next to me, some woman . . . is absolutely indignant when people tell her that there is an unbearable stench in the new rooms. "People in Lodz lived in worse conditions," she says. ■ One of the Jewish directors announces the happy news: "We might be moving back to the old block in an hour." The joy is indescribable. Here and there, there are only anxious questions about whether everyone will be allowed through. Feverishly, people start to set their appearances to rights. Everyone wants to look as "workmanlike" as possible. Men knot their ties and women put scarves on their heads and aprons over their dresses. I remember that, falling prey to the general psychosis, I go to the home of some friends and ask if I could have a head scarf and an apron. They tell me to take whatever I want. Their nicest and most expensive possessions are strewn on the floor and over the furniture. Generally, all the houses looked as if there has been a pogrom: people are feverishly ransacking their belongings, trying to pick out the most valuable things. . . . ■ The management tell us to stand in groups of fives. . . . ■ A large number of strangers (today's "barbarians") arrange themselves within the ranks of the "workshop." They want to slip through back to their old homes. The German proprietor of the factory announces that if a stranger is found amongst any of the fives, then everybody in that group will be removed. People are seized by fear. Questions are heard—"Do you have a pass?" "Who are you?" and so forth. Everybody moves away from the strangers as if from lepers. Amongst my group of five stands some woman who does not belong to our "workshop." She is pushed out of the team by force and one of our foremen, Fels, confirms that such so-called "local patriotism" is right because why should "our people" become victims for the sake of "strangers." . . . ■ From afar the ominous green uniforms of the SS are approaching. We are now standing on the corner of Niskia Street. . . . Next to us are gathering a group of people who work for the ▶

"The shoemaker's wife
wears no shoes."
–A Yiddish proverb.

Germans outside the ghetto, on the Ostbahn, I think. The men standing in the team show off their strength and vigor like slaves at a market. The majority are of an athletic build, wearing sportshirts and flexing their muscles. The German Werkschutz walk past, inspecting their slaves; I simply wait for the scene from *Uncle Tom's Cabin* where they examine their teeth like those of a horse. . . .
■ We move a few steps forward. It is difficult to move: the rucksacks chafe, children get underfoot, and it is scorchingly, sweltering hot. ■ We stop right on the corner of the street. The inspection has begun. It goes very quickly. I am quite far away and it is difficult for me to see what is going on. As we get closer to the control point, I can see the throng of people more clearly. On the right-hand side, the crowd grows larger and larger. There are women and children, very few men, but there are, above all, children. Now I can clearly pick out familiar faces. Ukrainians patrol in front of this group, which is destined for the railway wagons. More and more victims from the groups of five move in this direction. It is my group's turn. In front of me stands a young woman with a beautiful child in her arms. An SS officer's whip falls on her head. The officers of the Jewish police force quickly push her out of the team and her husband follows her. Some boy, pulled out of the team, calls out "Mummy!" His mother, who has been allowed through, is afraid to look back at her child. Exceptionally, there has been no shooting during our selection. It is said that in other places people dropped dead like flies. ■ Two SS officers inspect us. With whips in hand, of course. One moment—and sentence is passed. The whole group of five sets off at full tilt in the direction of the freed. They tell us to kneel. We kneel, one group of five behind the other. The SS men count us like cattle going to the slaughter. The company has been allocated 750 people. The Jewish police help with the counting. Never before have the Germans behaved like this toward the Jewish police during a raid. They beat them at every opportunity. To those of us who are kneeling, it seems as if we have already been through hell, but far from it!

At a certain moment, a German spots a child hidden amongst a group of five. He drags it out, together with the mother. Parallel with the kneeling teams are rows of carts and rickshaws with luggage. Porters stand next to the carts. At a certain moment, one of the Germans kicks a rickshaw. The suitcases fall off. From beneath the suitcases appears the figure of a boy of about five years old. An officer of the Jewish police profits from the inattention of the German and pushes the boy into a group of five between two girls loaded with rucksacks. The huge rucksacks hide the boy. It is worth pointing out that the Jewish police officer is the child's uncle. ■ We do not look behind us. We can only hear the shouts and the sobbing. A car stops beside us. The driver, also wearing the green uniform of the SS, gets out. His face, like that of all SS men, is terrible for the Jews. He speaks broken Polish, like a Prussian. He walks past us, looks sideways, a moment passes, and another victim tears herself from her knees and runs, driven by a whip, to the group of condemned people. Only women. People stop breathing. The driver searches a coat, which someone is holding next to me, checking to see that there is no child hidden there. He moves on. ■ The officers of the Jewish police bring the terrifying news: another thirty women are required from amongst the freed. And again we have to live through the torture of the fear that "maybe I. . . . " One weary figure after another rises and moves in the direction of death. . . . ■ Our knees hurt, the rucksacks weigh us down and our hearts beat weakly from anxiety: when will it be over, when will we go?
■ We simply cannot believe it when they tell us to get up. We walk along an empty Smocza Street. The street is terror-stricken. On both sides are the chairs used by the Jewish police, in the gutters lie brand new rucksacks, just used, stuffed, dropped by those who went to Treblinka. ■ We walk on. Already, from afar, we can see our gateway. We walk on, all of us: mothers without children, children without parents, husbands without wives. We have escaped death once more. ■ *Author unknown, Archives of the Jewish Historical Institute, Warsaw, translated from Polish.*

Half a million
Warsaw Jews and
refugees from
the provinces were
crowded into an
area of 1.36
square miles,
which included the
Jewish cemetery.

By the summer
of 1942, over
100,000 Jews
had died
in the ghetto.

The Umschlagplatz

At the Umschlagplatz, there is an escort and the shouts of the Germans. Slowly, the people walk further into the square, behind the wires; slowly, one after the other, they go into the empty rooms of the school building or remain out in the open. There is no water; there is not a bit of food to eat. People are alone, or sometimes with their families. They wait. The departure does not always take place at once. Usually, many hours pass, sometimes a day and a night, sometimes two. There are no trains. ■ They wait as the time passes. What for? Sometimes, for help from outside: maybe they will send some official, maybe those who remained will devise some salvation. Many people think like that, often rightly. But the majority, the vast majority, do not have anything or anyone to wait for. ■ And at the Umschlagplatz, in front of the wires, in the land of the free, there is some activity. A rickshaw draws up; officials of the Jewish police force and of the various Jewish Community Council departments arrive. Not everybody can come; a presence not justified by official duties can end badly. From being in front of the wires, one can end up behind them. Those who have a pretext come: an official from the Jewish police force—"on duty"; officials of the Health Department because their staff are on duty at the Umschlagplatz in the units supervising hygiene, bringing bread and water, moving sick people and bodies; officials of the Supply Establishment—in connection with the provision of food; officials of the Department of Hospital Management—on their way to the local hospital. An ambulance arrives; the white aprons of doctors and nurses appear. ■ [Those] who have a pretext come. All this activity has a single aim: to get one more person out from behind the wires, to free someone, to smuggle someone back. There are various ways, various methods of doing this: for money or without payment; in the aprons of the medical staff, amongst the shift returning to the ghetto; with the arm band and cap of a Jewish policeman; sometimes straight onto the "Aryan side" (through a hole in the wall); sometimes back to the ghetto; sometimes in some undertaker's wagon or cart. It is not an easy game; it is a difficult sport—is the merciless Szmerling on the alert? Many a time, the Germans discover these ruses and a bullet or the railway wagon—depending on the German's mood—is the reward for the person who wanted to exploit his privileged position "in a manner contrary to the law." And those behind the wire see the efforts, talk to those who want to save them and wait. They count the long minutes: Will they bring it off or not? Will there be a train today or not? ■ The crowd moves constantly; it is continually in motion. Some people slowly pace the rooms and corridors of the school building, or run ceaselessly up and down the stairs, through the halls and along the floors; others run across the square from one place to another, from the outer courtyard to the inner one and back again. ■ Here is the loaded railway wagon. . . . The latest scientific discovery allows eighty to one hundred people to be accommodated in one wagon. What if it is cramped, if death threatens from the crush or from the lack of air in the windowless wagons on a sweltering August day? What if these people suffocate? It is only a short distance, only a short journey, after all. These are only the temporary inconveniences of a summer trip. And the train slowly moves off. ■ *Jan Mawult,* All Are Equal, *Diary, Archives of the Jewish Historical Institute, Warsaw, translated from Polish.*

BOMBS At about midnight, I am awakened by the continuous wailing of a siren. It is the air-raid warning. After a moment, the continuous droning of the heavy bombers can be heard. A terrible bang rends the air. The explosions follow one another in quick succession. I take heart. Three years ago, I lived through the first raids. I was terribly afraid. They seemed to me then to be the height of cruelty. Not now. We have known cruelty far worse than this bombardment. It is better to be killed by a bomb than to die in the torments of Treblinka. At least this is familiar. . . . I do not hear around me, as I did then, the tears and the laments; I do not see the demented eyes, the faces mad with fright. Exactly the opposite. . . . There is a bitter joy . . . we are not alone . . . the explosions grow louder and louder. Nobody gets out of bed yet. Everyone lives with the strange belief that somehow they will not bomb the ghetto. . . . After all, they are friends. They will only bomb the German district or military targets. But Schultz, Toebbens, and the other factories are also military objectives. ■ My fellow tenant, a seamstress, daydreams about what she will do after the war. "You know, as soon as the war is over, the first thing I'm going to do is to eat my fill. At least once, I'm going to eat my fill. A whole loaf of white bread thickly buttered. And I'm not going stint myself the butter, oh no!" ■ Suddenly, a terrifying explosion rends the air . . . . A bomb has gone off somewhere very close by. Unfortunately, we have to get up and be ready in case something happens. In the courtyard and doorway, there are lots of people whispering to each other. "What could they be looking for here in the ghetto?" "And do you think that it is easy to hit the target from so high up?" ■ As if in reply, the whole building shakes to its very foundations. Nearly all the windowpanes fall out. From very nearby come shouts and groans, "Save us, save us!" ■ There is uncertainty on the pale faces. "Oh, it's all the same. Let them bomb the ghetto and destroy it. Anything's better than living like this. Let the end come at last. . . ." ■ "And yet, I would so like to live through all this. To survive until the end. To breathe freely again," declares an uncertain voice in the stillness of the night. "What do they want here?. . . Look how brightly they are lighting up the streets with flares. It's as clear as daylight. If only I were up there, I'd know what to bomb. I'd show them our oppressors. Destroy them all, turn them into a ruin. . . ." ■ Planes fly above our heads. There is hardly any doubt now that the ghetto is involved in the bombing to a very significant extent. ■ The shouts of "Save us, save us!" become clearer and clearer. It turns out that a splinter bomb has fallen on the adjoining house. The fragments have demolished the flats. There are dead and wounded. We run for help. There are no stretchers for the wounded, no bandages, no doctors. . . . And here, there are shouts, crying, groans. . . . We pull away the stones and rubble. . . . In the dark, trampling on bodies, we pull out the wounded, covered in blood. Nothing can equal the awfulness of that picture. There are already several dead. ■ There is disillusionment on the faces of the residents who have assembled and stand around as if turned to stone. "And we have had to bear so many casualties as well. After all, we have waited so long for that moment, for the moment when we would hear the droning of the planes, the explosions." ■ As if petrified, everyone looks at the bodies of the dead and wounded. They look and it is as if they cannot believe that what they see around them is reality. No, it is more of a misunderstanding. ■ Where did these bodies, groans and wails come from? . . . ■ How were these homes destroyed? . . . ■ The planes are above us again. But now people no longer wait with that unshakable confidence that no bomb will hit them. They run off in all directions. Everyone looks for his family so that they can keep together. . . . ■ The explosions now follow each other quickly. One after another, one after another. . . . The people try to guess where they are coming from. "If only the whole of the Umschlagplatz and the Transferstelle were bombed. . . ." "Yes, the Umschlagplatz, they should bomb the Umschlagplatz . . ." repeat the others. "But there are people in the railway wagons. . . ." "It's better to be killed by a bomb. It's a quicker end! . . ." ■ It is quiet at last. After about a quarter of an hour, the all-clear sounds. The raid has lasted two hours. The sky is lit up by the glow of the fires spread by the bombs. The silence of the night is broken by the ever-clearer groans and shouts: "Help! Save us!" ■ Why these casualties? How cruel is our fate. But, despite everything, it is easier to fall asleep now. Maybe it will really end? ■ It is odd. Where does this sudden hope come from? From one air raid, and are air raids in general to be the deciding factor in this war? Of course not! And yet the warm wave of faith embraces the heart and rocks it to a more serene sleep. Sleep peacefully, condemned person, the avenger is readying himself for the final reckoning with your executioner. ■ *Emanuel Ringelblum, Notes from the Warsaw Ghetto, Archives of the Jewish Historical Institute, Warsaw, translated from Polish.*

Himmler
Reichsführer SS Field Command
Journal No. 38/33/43 g.
February 16, 1943
Secret!

To: Higher SS and Police Leader
(Hoher SS und Polizeiführer),
East SS Obergruppenführer Kurger,
Cracow

■ For reasons of security, I herewith order
that the Warsaw Ghetto be pulled down
after the concentration camp has been
moved: all parts of houses that can be
used, and other materials of all kinds,
are first to be made use of. ■ The razing
of the ghetto and the relocation of the
concentration camp are necessary, as
otherwise we would probably never estab-
lish quiet in Warsaw, and the prevalence
of crime cannot be stamped out as long as
the ghetto remains. ■ An overall plan for
the razing of the ghetto is to be submitted
to me. In any case, we must achieve the
disappearance from sight of the living
space for 500,000 subhumans
(Untermenschen) that has existed up to
now, but could never be suitable for
Germans, and reduce the size of this city
of millions—Warsaw—which has always
been a center of corruption and revolt.

■ signed H. Himmler

Blood-splattered Stones A layer of snow glistens and shimmers in the glow of an unequaled, golden Polish autumn. This "snow" is nothing but the feathers and down from bedding left behind, along with all their possessions from wardrobes, trunks, and suitcases full of bedding and clothes to bowls, pots, plates, and other household goods, by the 500,000 Jews evacuated to the East. The ownerless objects—tablecloths, coats, quilts, sweaters, books, cradles, papers, photographs—lie piled in heaps about the houses, courtyards, and squares, covered by that "snow" from the time of the greatly stepped-up German slaughter of the Jews of Warsaw, covered by the disemboweled innards of their bedding. ■ The eerie silence is broken by revolver shots, the rattle of light machine guns, the droning of car and motorcycle engines from the German patrols, the crack of doors and furniture being broken up, the hoarse shouts of "Alle Juden raus" ("All Jews out"), the macabre march of the Jewish victims condemned to death, and the rhythmic beating against the paving stones of the boots of the international band of Fascists—Lithuanians, Latvians, Ukrainians—and of the ghetto police under the direction of SS officers. The deserted or moribund buildings, the streets full of barbed-wire entanglements, the wooden hoardings used to divide up the blocks of communal flats and, above all, the complete absence of people who two months ago still filled the main streets of the ghetto, hurrying about their everyday business, buying and selling—a depopulation unknown even in the age of the Black Death and the plagues—this is the picture of the Jewish district of Warsaw in September 1942. The scrap of humanity moving stealthily along the walls, the blood-splattered stones of the pavement, the smoke rising from the smoldering and dying street fires, the acrid smell of burning, all add an air of authenticity to this city of death where, prior to that terrible August 22, almost 370,000 Jews rotted within the ten-kilometer radius of the walls surrounding the ghetto. ■ *Report to the Polish government in London from the Polish Underground, translated from Polish.*

Sing!   "Sing! Take your light, hollow harp in hand,
Strike hard with heavy fingers, like pain-filled hearts
On its thin chords. Sing the last song.
Sing of the last Jews on Europe's soil."

—How can I sing? How can I open my lips?
I who am left alone in the wilderness—
My wife, my two children, alas!
I shudder . . . Someone's crying! I hear it from afar.

"Sing, sing! Raise your tormented and broken voice,
Look for Him, look up, if He is still there—
Sing to Him . . . Sing Him the last song of the last Jew,
Who lived, died unburied, and is no more."

—How can I sing? How can I lift my head?
My wife, my Benzionke and Yomele—a baby—deported . . .
They are not with me, yet they never leave me.
O dark shadows of my brightest lights, O cold, blind shadows!

"Sing, sing for the last on earth.
Throw back your head; fix your eyes upon Him.
Sing to Him for the last time, play to Him on your harp:
There are no more Jews! They were killed, they are no more."

—How can I sing? How can I lift my head
With bleary eyes? A frozen tear
Clouds my eye . . . It struggles to break loose,
But God, my God, it cannot fall!

"Sing, sing! Raise your eyes toward the high, blind skies
As if a God were there . . . Beckon to Him—
As if a great joy still shone for us there!
Sit on the ruins of the murdered people and sing!"

—How can I sing? My world is laid waste.
How can I play with wringed hands?
Where are my dead? O God, I seek them in every dunghill,
In every heap of ashes . . . O tell me where you are.

Awake and Fight! We are rising up for war!

We are of those who have set themselves the aim of awakening the people. Our wish is to take this watchword to our people:

■ Awake and fight!

■ Do not despair of the road to escape!

Know that escape is not to be found by walking to your death passively, like sheep to the slaughter. It is to be found in something much greater: in war!

Whoever defends himself has a chance of being saved! Whoever gives up self-defense from the outset—he has lost already! Nothing awaits him except a hideous death in the suffocation-machine of Treblinka.

■ Let the people awaken to war!

Find the courage in your soul for desperate action! Put an end to our terrible acceptance of such phrases as: We are all under sentence of death!

It is a lie!!!

We also were destined to live! We too have a right to life! One only needs to know how to fight for it!

It is no great art to live when life is given to you willingly! But there is an art to life just when they are trying to rob you of this life.

■ Let the people awaken and fight for its life!

Let every mother be a lioness defending her young!

Let no father stand by and see the blood of his children in silence!

Let not the first act of our destruction be repeated!

An end to despair and lack of faith!

An end to the spirit of slavery amongst us!

■ *Call for resistance by the Jewish Military Organization in the Warsaw Ghetto, January 1943, translated from Polish.*

Scream from every sand dune, from under every stone,
Scream from the dust and fire and smoke—
It is your blood, your sap, the marrow of your bones,
It is your flesh and blood! Scream, scream aloud!

Scream from the beasts' entrails in the wood,
from the fish in the river
That devoured you. Scream from furnaces.
Scream, young and old.

Do not scream to heaven that is as deaf as the dunghill earth.
Do not scream to the sun, nor talk to that lamp . . . If I could only
Extinguish it like a lamp in this bleak murderers' cave!
My people, you were radiant more that the sun,
a purer, brighter light!

Show yourself, my people. Emerge, reach out
From the miles-long, dense, deep ditches,
Covered with lime and burned, layer upon layer,
Rise up! Up! From the deepest, bottommost layer!

Come from Treblinka, Sobibor, Auschwitz,
Come from Belzec, Ponari, from all the other camps,
With wide open eyes, frozen cries and soundless screams.
Come from marshes, deep sunken swamps, foul moss—

Come, you dried, ground, crushed Jewish bones.
Come, form a big circle around me, one great ring—
Grandfathers, grandmothers, fathers, mothers carrying babies.
Come, Jewish bones, out of powder and soup.

Emerge, reveal yourselves to me. Come, all of you, come.
I want to see you, I want to look at you. I want
Silently and mutely to behold my murdered people—
And I will sing . . . Yes . . . Hand me the harp . . . I will play!

■ *Yitzhak Kacenelson, "The Song of the Murdered
Jewish People," The Ghetto Fighters House, Israel; translated
from Yiddish by Noah H. Rosenbloom.*

When the German army entered Warsaw on September 20, 1939, nearly 400,000 Jews were living in the city, roughly a third of the population. Immediately, they became the target of mounting repression—subjected to forced labor, prohibited from using railways and other public transport, made to wear the Star of David, stripped of their possessions. Virtually without protection of the law, they fell to the mercy of hooligans, sadists, and robbers, of whom there was no shortage. The daily food ration for Warsaw's Jews became 184 calories, compared with 669 for a Pole and 2,613 for a German. ■ On October 2, 1940, the Germans established an area into which all Warsaw Jews—roughly 138,000 people—along with persons of Jewish origin and Jewish refugees from the provinces were herded; some 113,000 "Aryans" living in that area had to leave. The Germans then declared the district a "plague-infested" zone, and the Jews were required to build a wall around it. ■ The Germans did not like the word "ghetto" and forbade its use; they referred to it as the "Jewish residential district" (*Wohnbezirk*). Indeed, the comparison with a medieval ghetto is totally inappropriate, as it implies a degree of normalcy, where people were born, pursued their interests, died in their beds. In that "district," surrounded by a ten-foot-high wall and a parapet of barbed wire, in a space of approximately 1,000 acres, a population of about 500,000 had to sustain itself, thirteen persons to a room, and many thousands without a roof over their heads. Nearly 60 percent of the population was left without a means of making a living. ■ In Warsaw, as in other occupied towns, the Germans designated a *Judenrat* (Jewish council) as the body responsible—with their own lives—for the enforcement of orders in the Jewish community. After the establishment of the ghettos, the *Judenrat* was given control of the police, economic management, and all matters of food supply, housing, and education. Although this seemed to be giving Jews a great deal of managerial autonomy, in reality the Germans created the *Judenrat* solely for their own convenience. *Judenrat* members had no option whatsoever but to respond to every command or caprice of their masters. They were often charged with collecting punitive contributions, one method of reducing the Jewish population to penury. As might be expected—and this indeed was part of the German plan—the *Judenrat* often attracted the fierce hostility and hatred of the Jewish population, deflecting these emotions from the real executioners. The role of the *Judenrat* remains a subject of controversy in the study of the behavior of Jews under German occupation. ■ The Germans appointed Adam Czerniakow as head of the Warsaw *Judenrat*—it mattered little to them who would act as their puppet. Czerniakow kept a diary in which he noted his daily dealings with various German officials—a diary that remains a most important source of knowledge of that period. It shows Czerniakow, much maligned by his contemporaries, as an almost heroic figure, pleading and arguing with his implacable masters with great courage and dignity, wringing from them small concessions here and there, trying to persuade himself and those around him, in the face of mounting evidence to the contrary, that the worst would not happen. When it became clear, even to him, that "resettlement" was a euphemism for murder, he refused to put his signature to a directive ordering the deportation of children, and took his own life. He was condemned by many as a coward, and his contemporaries comment bitterly in their diaries: he should have warned the ghetto, he should have issued a call for resistance. Later judgments are kinder to him. This points to the agonizing moral dilemmas that often faced people in those apocalyptic times, dilemmas to which there was and is no answer. ■ The Warsaw Ghetto was a vast concentration camp with a simple ultimate purpose—to exterminate the Jews through hunger, through cold, through disease. As time went on, it became common to see corpses on the street. Bands of children roamed the alleyways searching for food scraps. Even though the gates were guarded and the penalty for leaving the ghetto without permission was death, the residents tried to survive by smuggling food from the outside. Risking their lives, children proved the most effective smugglers and supporters of their families. ■ The German governor, Hans Frank, stated in a report, "It is not necessary to dwell on the fact that we are sentencing the Jews to death. If the Jews do not die of starvation, it will be necessary to step up anti-Jewish measures, and let us hope that, too, will come to pass." Frank's vision soon materialized in the fulfillment of the Wannsee Conference decision on the "Final Solution." In July 1942, under the pretext of "resettlement," a mass deportation to the death camps began and continued, with short pauses, until mid September. During those seven weeks some 265,000 Jews were transported to Treblinka and murdered in the gas chambers. Some of the victims, lured by the promise of food, presented themselves voluntarily at the Umschlagplatz—the railway siding from which the human cargo was packed into cattle trucks and dispatched to the death camps. The deportation drastically reduced the ghetto population; 35,000 inhabitants were permitted to stay—mainly workers employed in German workshops and their families. In addition, some 25,000 Jews were hiding in the ghetto illegally. ■ Under such conditions, as a defiant gesture and in a quixotic attempt "to die as human beings," Jews organized a resistance. A few hundred desperate people, gathered from the whole spectrum of Jewish society, formed battle units, arming themselves with a few pistols, submachine guns, and Molotov cocktails. In all, their defense amounted to very little. On April 19, 1943, when German troops entered the ghetto to finally liquidate the last remnants of the population, they met with armed resistance. To their surprise and shock, the Jewish fighters inflicted losses on them and forced them to retreat. The outcome of the battle was, of course, never in doubt for a moment. General Juergen Stroop crushed the uprising with tanks, heavy artillery, and flame-throwers. Avoiding open street combat, he systematically burned the houses, block by block. German bombs and hand grenades killed the fighters huddled in bunkers and canals. In spite of that, the battle continued sporadically until May 8, 1943. As a final, triumphant act in the war against the Jews, General Stroop blew up the Great Synagogue in Warsaw and wrote in his report: "The Jewish residential district is no more." ■ The Warsaw Ghetto uprising had an enormous effect on the morale of the Jews and non-Jews around the world. The longest battle against the Germans in occupied Europe before April 1943, the uprising story has become a legend. ■ We owe a great deal of our knowledge of that period to the effort and initiative of one man, Emanuel Ringelblum (1900–1944). A teacher, historian, and social worker, he is one of the unsung heroes of our time. From the initial outbreak of war, he became one of the chief organizers of Warsaw self-help and mutual assistance committees. He kept a chronicle of

events and, at his inspiration, in the autumn of 1940, a group with the cryptonym "Oneg Shabbat" (The joy of the Sabbath) started writing bulletins describing and documenting the situation. Under his guidance, Oneg Shabbat developed a network of reporters all over the country who collected information in response to a prepared questionnaire. They thought, rightly, that every scrap of paper relating to Jewish life would be of inestimable historical value. Thus they collected official posters, public announcements, diaries, letters, advertisements, packaging, copies of the monitored foreign radio broadcasts and, above all, newspapers and news sheets of the many underground groupings. They commissioned special reports on various aspects of life and fed news items to the Polish underground press. ■ The Germans took little interest at first in what the Jews were doing among themselves. Jews could write, talk, curse, and gossip almost openly. They could discuss in the streets and cafés the illegal news sheets that circulated freely in the ghetto. Semiofficial and clandestine committees sustained the fabric of communal life on all levels, alleviating hunger, providing education, organizing cultural events, setting up projects for medical research, generally keeping up the spirits and the morale of the population. Behind the facades of the tenement houses, around the large, typical Warsaw courtyards, cultural and religious life took on new forms adapted to the unprecedented, immediate needs. ■ The network of the Oneg Shabbat was the first to obtain eyewitness reports of the mass murders by gas in Chelmno, the first to raise the alarm in the Polish underground press and, finally, abroad. On June 26, 1942, the BBC broadcast news of the extermination of Polish Jews, based on reports sent by Ringelblum. He noted: "By alerting the world to our fate we fulfilled a great, historic mission. Maybe this will save some hundreds of thousands of Polish Jews. The near future will show. I don't know which one of our group will remain alive, whom fate will choose to make use of our archives, but of one thing we are certain— that our sacrifices, the risks taken, the tension of constant danger, our toil and suffering, have not been in vain." ■ As the noose tightened, the danger of losing the archives caused serious concern. A few months before the liquidation of the ghetto, all materials were assembled, packed into sealed milk churns and metal containers and buried in a cellar deep under the ghetto buildings. After the war, in 1946 and 1950, two parts of the treasure were found under the mountain of rubble which was all that remained of the ghetto. The third part must be considered beyond retrieval, and the sense of its loss is haunting. ■ The recovered collection consists of some forty thousand pages, mostly still awaiting analysis and publication. The largest and the most important archive of the era, it remains a priceless source of what we currently know and may yet know about the life and death of the Warsaw Ghetto and the destruction of Polish Jews. ■ Ringelblum gave of himself unstintingly to the last. In March 1943 he was persuaded to leave the ghetto and find shelter on the "Aryan side." On April 18, the day before the last deportation and the eve of the ghetto uprising, he reentered the ghetto, wishing to spend Passover with the last survivors. He was caught in a roundup and sent to a concentration camp near Lublin. When his location became known, a team smuggled him out of the camp and brought him back to his Warsaw hiding place, reuniting him with his wife and son. He continued writing; amazingly, without access to books and sources, he wrote one of his key studies, *The Relations Between Poles and Jews in the Second World War.* ■ In March 1944 the Gestapo discovered Ringelblum's hiding place, which reputedly housed 60 people. All of the Jews and the Polish family who sheltered them were taken to the Pawiak prison and shot—within a stone's throw of the ghetto. ■ In one respect, at least, the Germans were unlucky in their choice of victims. The Jewish people were determined to leave a trace of their fate, at whatever cost. Feeling abandoned by God and man, they were haunted by the thought that the world would not know how they lived and died. Writing made dying easier. The last entry in Chaim Kaplan's diary before his deportation to Treblinka was his anguished cry: "If I die—what will happen to my diary?" ■ Primo Levi, in *The Drowned and the Saved,* imagines members of the SS taunting their victims: "However this war may end, we have won the war against you, none of you will be left to bear witness, and even if someone were to survive, the world would not believe him. There will perhaps be suspicions, discussions, research by historians, but here will be no certainties, because we will destroy the evidence together with you. And even if some proof should remain and

some of you survive, people will say that the events you describe are too monstrous to be believed; they will say that they are exaggerations of Allied propaganda and will believe us, who will deny everything, and not you." ■ Because of these writers and scribblers, the truth has been recorded, has become known to the world, and no one but a maniac or pervert will deny it. These testimonies give us a picture of consummately hideous times. They show us the depth to which humans can descend, and they document how hatred can bring hell on this earth. ■ In putting together this volume, I chose to limit the selections presented to writing actually done at the time in the ghetto. On a few occasions, I admit excerpts from writing done later but based on notes written outside the ghetto walls soon after their authors escaped to the "Aryan side." ■ The task of selecting the passages has been harrowing; human sensibility is numbed by the horror and pity of it all. Even though these testimonies relate to events of half a century ago, their immediacy is such that they tend to mark the reader for life. I certainly feel I have been marked thus. ■ The photographs on the preceding pages were handed to me by Willy Georg, a former soldier in the German army, to whose doorstep I was led by friends who knew of my consuming interest in this field. Willy Georg is now over eighty years old—of a generation of Germans with whom I am not at ease without further probing. I am satisfied that he is not suspect: a man of good education and a fairly prosperous background, a professional photographer; at the age of thirty, when these photographs were taken, he was still in the humble rank of *Funke*—a radio operator. This does not point to someone who was favored by or benefited from membership in the Nazi party. ■ How did these photographs come to be taken? Willy Georg has a clear recollection. He was stationed with his unit in Warsaw (in a district called Mokotow, he thinks). Known to his colleagues and superiors as a professional photographer, he was earning extra money to send home by taking snapshots of his fellow soldiers. One day, in summer of 1941, his officer called him and said, lightheartedly: "There are some curious goings-on behind that wall. I am issuing you with a pass to enter the enclosed area through one of the gates. Take your Leica, and food for the day, and bring back some photos of what you find." ■ He did as he was told. He entered the ghetto, walked around, snapped what he saw on four rolls of film, loaded the fifth. Toward evening a German police detachment entered the ghetto, spotted him, and told him to hand over the camera. They opened the back and removed the film; Georg said nothing about the four rolls in his pocket. His credentials verified, he was led outside the gates. He developed the film himself in a photo laboratory in Warsaw. He is proud of his professionalism: after half a century, the film looks as crisp as new. He sent the film home, to his wife in Munster. He gave it little thought in the intervening years, until lately, when he felt the time was approaching to make his final dispositions. ■ He felt shocked to the core, he says, when he saw these photos anew and recalled those times. It would have been tempting to ask him how he felt then, fifty years ago, when he came, unprepared, upon that horrific scene, unlike anything he could have encountered before. But there would have been no point in this: all he would have said is what he thinks of it now, or, rather, what he thinks would be appropriate to say to me now. He remembers how polite these people were to him. Although he might not have known it, they had to be polite: a Jew encountering a German was obliged by order to doff his cap and step off the pavement.

■ This photographic record is not unprecedented. Other photographs still exist that were taken in the ghetto by the Germans around that time and later. (The most famous image—of a small boy in a peaked cap, with his hands raised—stems from one such source.) A team from the German Propaganda Ministry assembled a collection that is now in the official German archives in Koblenz. These photographs were made with the explicit purpose of showing the degradation of that subhuman race, of their indifference to the suffering of their brethren (look how they pass the corpses lying on the street without batting an eyelid!), of people allegedly enjoying themselves playing cards in coffeehouses. These photographers and their masters were clearly unaware of the reverse effect of their work—ultimately, the images degrade not the victims but those who created them. ■ Willy Georg's snapshots, on the other hand, were totally spontaneous; they simply record the passing scene. The people caught in these photographs—busy, feverish, emaciated, oppressed, but still living a life of sorts—are unaware of the unthinkably cruel end that awaits them shortly. Virtually none will escape a horrible death. One's instinct is to shout a word of warning—run! hide!—but it is too late. At that stage nothing, but nothing, they could have done or left undone would have had the slightest effect on their fate ■ To many of us who grew up within or next to that human landscape and who remember it lovingly, these people—shameful to confess—did not at that time look attractive. These misty eyes, beards, sidelocks, crooked noses—one looked away, embarrassed by what a non-Jewish onlooker might feel or say. It now seems clear that these faces, etched with worry and wisdom, lit with inner light, otherwordly, Rembrandtesque, were inexpressibly beautiful. Set against that rogue's gallery, the flower of the "master race"—Goebbels, Goering, Striecher, Frank, and Hitler himself—little more need be said. ■ These photographs give a last glimpse of a people to be murdered, leaving the world forever and irreparably the poorer for it. The lessons of their lives become more valuable as the time approaches when there will be no living witnesses, and future generations might find such things beyond belief.

Book design, jacket, and text composition by Peter Bradford and Danielle Whiteson. Photographs printed by Yetish Center of Photography. Separations, printing and binding by Arti Grafiche Motta SPA, Milan, Italy.

THE STAFF AT APERTURE for *In the Warsaw Ghetto: Summer, 1941* is Michael E. Hoffman, Executive Director; Rebecca Busselle, Editor; Michael Sand, Managing Editor; Stevan A. Baron, Production Director; Sandra Greve, Production Associate; Jenny Isaacs, Work Scholar.

Aperture publishes a periodical, books and portfolios of fine photography to communicate with serious photographers and creative people everywhere. A complete catalog is available upon request.

Address: 20 East 23rd Street, New York, New York 10010.

First edition

ACKNOWLEDGMENTS My thanks to Oswald Burstin for the encouragement he offered when my resolve was flagging; to Joanna Michlic-Coren, whose range of reading and sensitive judgment made the task of selecting the texts endurable; to Jane Kleiner for her manifold skills as reader and translator; to Abrasha Sarid of the Ghetto Fighters' Kibbutz for good guidance; above all to my wife for bearing with me when my mind, all too often, dwelt more on the past than on the present.
— *Rafael F. Scharf*

The Aperture Foundation would like to thank the Samuel Bronfman Foundation for its generous support and the following for their guidance and encouragement:

Dr. Lucjan Dobroszycki, historian, YIVO and Yeshiva University; editor, *The Chronicle of the Lodz Ghetto*

Boleck and Anna Ellenbogen, survivors, the Warsaw Ghetto

Michael Estorick, London

Rabbi Philip Hiat, Senior Consultant, Union of American Hebrew Congregations; Scholar-in-Residence, Central Synagogue, New York City

Benjamin Meed, President, Warsaw Ghetto Resistance Organization